Asher's Little Talk With Yah:
A Hebrew Child's Prayer

By: Jennifer S Williams

Copyright © 2019 Jennifer S Williams

All rights reserved.

ISBN: 9781072334651

DEDICATION

Being an Israelite, a child of The Most High, is not strictly defined based on bloodline. As a Hebrew I understand that my birthright is extremely important for many reasons, however I believe that being a child of The Most High is not about religion or genealogy. I believe it is about relationship and the way we worship.

I pray this story inspires ALL believers and followers of HaMashiac Yahusha (The Anointed One many call Jesus Christ) to learn more about your Hebraic based faith. Learn the about the people, the culture, and the language. Learn more about the Elohim (God) of the Hebrews, his redemption plan and how He wants His covenant keeping children to worship.

"There is one law for the citizen and for the stranger who lives among you.... One Lord, one Faith, one baptism. One God who is Father of us all, who is above all and through all and in you all." This promise belongs to me and my children, to you and your children and to all who are afar off, to whom Yahuah our Elohim (God) will call to himself.

"Blessed be the name of Yahuah from this time forth and forevermore."

Exodus 12:49; Numbers15:15; Leviticus 18:26; Acts2:39; Isaiah 14:1; Isaiah 56; Isaiah 49:15; Isaiah 54; Ephesians 3:6; Ezekiel 47:22; Colossians1:21; Acts 15: 19-29; Psalms 113:2

ACKNOWLEDGMENTS

Matthew, thank you for walking with me on this journey called life, for all of your encouragement and all of your love . The love of Christ truly lives inside you! I love you!

Caleb and Kalen, my bonus babies, thank you for welcoming me into your lives with an abundance of love. You are the best big brothers Asher and Ezra could ask for. I love you!

Asher Langston and Ezra Gabriel, my first born and my baby, I learn so much from you. You are the greatest gifts The Most High has entrusted me with! You've changed my life for the better and you inspire me daily to be the best version of myself. I pray you always remember to keep Yah first in your life.... "Seek first the Kingdom of Yah and His righteousness and ALL THINGS will be added to you."

This book is for you!

I'm so proud to be your mommy! I love you!

ASHER'S LITTLE TALK WITH YAH

A Hebrew Child's Prayer

BY JENNIFER WILLIAMS

One night before bed Asher went to his mommy and said "Mommy, I want to pray like you. I just don't know what to say or what to do. Can you teach me how to pray?"

His mommy replied, "There are many ways to pray. Many ways to lift Yah's name both night and day. I'll share with you a few tips to help you along the way.

Bow down to show respect. Bless Yah's name, He exists, this is something we do not neglect.

Thank Him for your blessings in advance, every time you have a chance.

Ask to forgive. Ask to show mercy and love. Ask Yah for what you are in need of.

Ask for wisdom, ask for strength. Ask Yah for any perfect gift.

Never mind what you see; it matters what you believe. Believe in His promises, believe in His truth. Stand firm in your belief and Yah will surely bless you.

The fruit you wish to grow indeed will happen if you plant the seed.

"Remember," mom exclaimed, "we serve the King of Kings! He has much to spare."

"You mean whatever I ask in prayer, the Father will provide? It will be there?" questioned Asher.

"One of His promises is this, and all of His promises are true," said mommy, "whatever you ask with faith and in His name, he said he will do.

Now faith is more than simply saying you believe. Even the enemy believes, but he continues to deceive.

Faith alone is dead, without good deeds. Good behavior is a start, but often times we miss the mark.

In your prayer ask for forgiveness and admit to Yah your mistakes. Only because of His loving kindness does our Father in Heaven give us mercy and grace.

Torah is our God given instruction. When we listen and obey we avoid the coming destruction.

Torah teaches us to aim and live our best life. The Prophets proclaim the Righteous One, who made the ultimate sacrifice. His name is Yahusha. Some people call him Jesus Christ.

He was perfect. Never did he make a mistake. He was kind, patient, wise and filled with love every day.

He laid down his perfect life so that you and I could live. His righteous blood washed away our sins so the Father in heaven would forgive.

But this did not bring an end to the law and prophets, like some might say. It allowed us to be Yah's friend again and walk righteously in the way.

Yahusha came to fully walk out the Torah, live and fulfill. After his death, burial and resurrection, he left us Ruach HaKodesh (The Holy Spirit), as our power to overcome sin and as our seal.

To be in Christ means, in you, Yah's

Set Apart Spirit is instilled. You show your faith by acting in accordance with His will.

Now ask your prayer in the name and character of Yahusha. Yah is our salvation, our Messiah and ruler.

Keep your mind on heavenly things, things that come from above; like justice, mercy, forgiveness and love.

These are the things that Yah delights in the most. Be humble when you speak and never boast.

Be strong and courageous. Do not fear. Remember my child you have Him near.

If you ever wonder or you just don't

know, Yah loves you and He is with you wherever you go."

The End

SCRIPTURE REFRENCES/PROMISES:

<u>Kneel down, Bless His name</u>
Nehemiah 8:6
1 Chronicles 29:20
Psalms 95:5
Ephesians 3:14
James 4:10

<u>Be Thankful</u>
Psalms 106:1
1 Thessalonians 5:18
Colossians 4:2
Philippians 4:6

<u>Forgiveness, Mercy, Love</u>
Mark 11:25
Ephesians 4:32
2 Samuel 22:26
Luke 6:36
Proverbs 3: 3-4
Leviticus 19:18
Matthew 5: 44-45

<u>Wisdom, Strength, Gifts</u>
Proverbs 9:10
Proverbs 4:6-7
Ecclesiastes 2:26
James 3:17
James 1:5
Philippians 4:13
Isaiah 40:31
James 1:17
Ephesians 2:8

<u>Believe in His Truth, Stand Firm.</u>
2 Timothy 3:16
Psalms 119:160
Psalms 119:142
Ephesians 1:13
1 Peter 5:9

Asher's Little Talk With Yah: A Hebrew Child's Prayer

ABOUT THE AUTHOR

Jennifer S Williams, a child of The Most High, mother of Asher and Ezra and Founder of Kingdom Kids Academy Inc learned she had a passion for creating at an early age. Growing up as a military child consistently moving and often feeling estranged, her solace was found in reading and creative writing. Inspired by fairy tale stories, her imagination began to develop as she displayed her talents by writing poems and stories of her own, often acting out scenes while playing "make believe" with her stuffed animals and dolls.

Jennifer received a full academic scholarship to Wiley College to study Business Administration and later transferred to Indiana University Bloomington obtaining a Bachelors of Arts in Telecommunication Management. She is now the founder/owner of Kingdom Kids Academy Inc where she incorporates education, imagination, and Torah inspired values to help teach and mold young children into the image of Yahusha.

Asher's Little Talk With Yah: A Hebrew Child's Prayer

CPSIA information can be obtained
at www.ICGtesting.com
Printed in the USA
LVHW091602170322
713580LV00005B/569